WHY DO WE CALL PLUTO A DWARF?

Astronomy Book Best Sellers
Children's Astronomy Books

In this book, we're going to talk about one of the dwarf planets in our Solar System, the planet Pluto. So, let's get right to it!

WHAT IS PLUTO?

At one time, Pluto was considered to be the ninth planet in our Solar System and the farthest from the Sun. At the current time, it's categorized as the largest of the dwarf planets. This re-classification of the planet happened in 2006. The decision has been debated and discussed since then and it may be overturned in the future.

The reason this occurred is because after much debate, astronomers redefined what a planet is. Here are the reasons a celestial body is categorized as a planet:

- It orbits the Sun.

- It's large enough that it's generally a sphere in shape.

- It is the largest object in the neighborhood of its orbit.

Pluto definitely orbits the Sun and it's spherical in shape. However, Pluto is in the Kuiper Belt. This zone is past Neptune's orbit. The Kuiper Belt has leftover frozen objects from when the Solar System was being formed. These objects are made of the same type of ices as the "ice planets." Pluto, lots of other dwarf planets, and hundreds of thousands of other rocky objects are there as well.

WHO DISCOVERED PLUTO?

Astronomer Percival Lowell was the first person to believe that there was another object influencing the orbits of both Neptune and Uranus. He was studying their orbits and noticed that something else was tugging at them.

PERCIVAL LOWELL IN 1914

CLYDE TOMBAUGH

He predicted that there was another body's gravitational pull causing it. He studied these orbits for ten years and predicted where the other object would be in 1915, but he passed away without finding Pluto. Based on Lowell's predictions, Pluto was finally seen in 1930 by astronomer Clyde Tombaugh at the observatory named after Lowell.

HOW DID PLUTO GET ITS NAME?

Venetia Burney, an 11-year-old girl, came up with the name for the dwarf planet. She was talking with her grandfather over breakfast about the news of its discovery, when she came up with the idea.

PLUTO'S ATMOSPHERE

ROMAN GOD PLUTO

Her grandfather sent a telegram to a friend of his that was an astronomer. His friend sent a telegraph to Lowell Observatory, where the name was considered, debated, and then adopted. It was named Pluto after the Roman god Pluto. Pluto reigned over the underworld so the name seemed appropriate for a dark, lifeless planet. The first two letters of the word "Pluto" also honored Percival Lowell.

HOW BIG IS PLUTO?

Pluto is very far away from Earth. The unmanned spacecraft New Horizons flew close to Pluto in 2015. It had taken a journey of almost 10 years to get to the distant dwarf planet. Data was collected and it was found that Pluto is about 1,400 miles across. That means it is only about 20% of the Earth's diameter.

NEW HORIZONS PLUTO ENCOUNTER

MOUNTAINS AND PLAINS

COMPOSITION AND STRUCTURE

Scientists already knew that Pluto had an icy composition but NASA's New Horizons mission brought back a lot more details about the surface of the dwarf planet. It showed that Pluto had mountain ranges that are as high as the Rocky Mountains on our planet.

Since ice made of nitrogen and methane wrap Pluto's surface, scientists believe that the mountains are built up on frozen water, since nitrogen and methane ice aren't strong enough. Water, even frozen water, is always an important finding.

Another finding, this time from NASA's Hubble Telescope, indicates that its crust could contain organic molecules, important substances needed for life.

cientists believe that Pluto's inner core is rocky with surrounding layers of ice made of water. Ices from the elements of methane as well as nitrogen and carbon monoxide are on the outermost surface. Its composition is more than likely about 70% rocky structure and about 30% of different types of ice.

Pluto has an atmosphere made up of nitrogen and methane gases. Its atmosphere goes up as far as 1,000 miles above the dwarf planet's surface. It extends so far up because Pluto doesn't have much gravity compared to larger bodies. As far as astronomers know, Pluto has no significant magnetic field.

THE "HEART" OF PLUTO

There is a large area on Pluto's surface that looks like a heart. It's called Tombaugh Regio after the astronomer Clyde Tombaugh. It's made by nitrogen ice that forms in its basin. Another interesting surface feature is the Sputnik Planum, after the historic artificial satellite Sputnik.

TOMBAUGH REGIO

Astronomers are very excited by its discovery. This area has no craters from the impact of meteorites. This means that the surface hasn't been around too long. It's quite "young" at least in geologic time. They believe it's only about 100 million years old.

The plains of ice on Pluto have dark streaks going through them. Scientists are not sure, but they believe that these might be caused by very strong wings whipping across Pluto's surface.

ARTIST'S CONCEPT OF THE PLUTO SYSTEM

TEMPERATURE ON PLUTO

At minus 375 degrees Fahrenheit, Pluto's surface is unbelievably cold. Even with the cold temperatures, Hubble's photos show that there may be seasons on Pluto since at times it looks redder.

GRAVITY ON PLUTO

Can you dunk a basketball into a 10-foot tall basket on Earth? If the answer is yes, then you could do that on Pluto too, for a basket that was 150 feet tall! The reason is that the gravity on Pluto is so much less than Earth's gravity. It's not because you'd be a better basketball player.

PLUTO AND CHARON

ORBIT AND ROTATION

The Earth takes 365 days to orbit the Sun. One year on Pluto takes 248 Earth years! So if you lived on Pluto and you were only one year old as measured by Pluto's time, you'd be 248 years old on Earth's time.

Pluto's orbit around the Sun is so elliptical that at times it's closer to the Sun than the planet Neptune is. That occurs for 20 years during its 248 year cycle, as measured by Earth years. When the dwarf planet is closer to the Sun, it gives astronomers a better chance to study it by telescope.

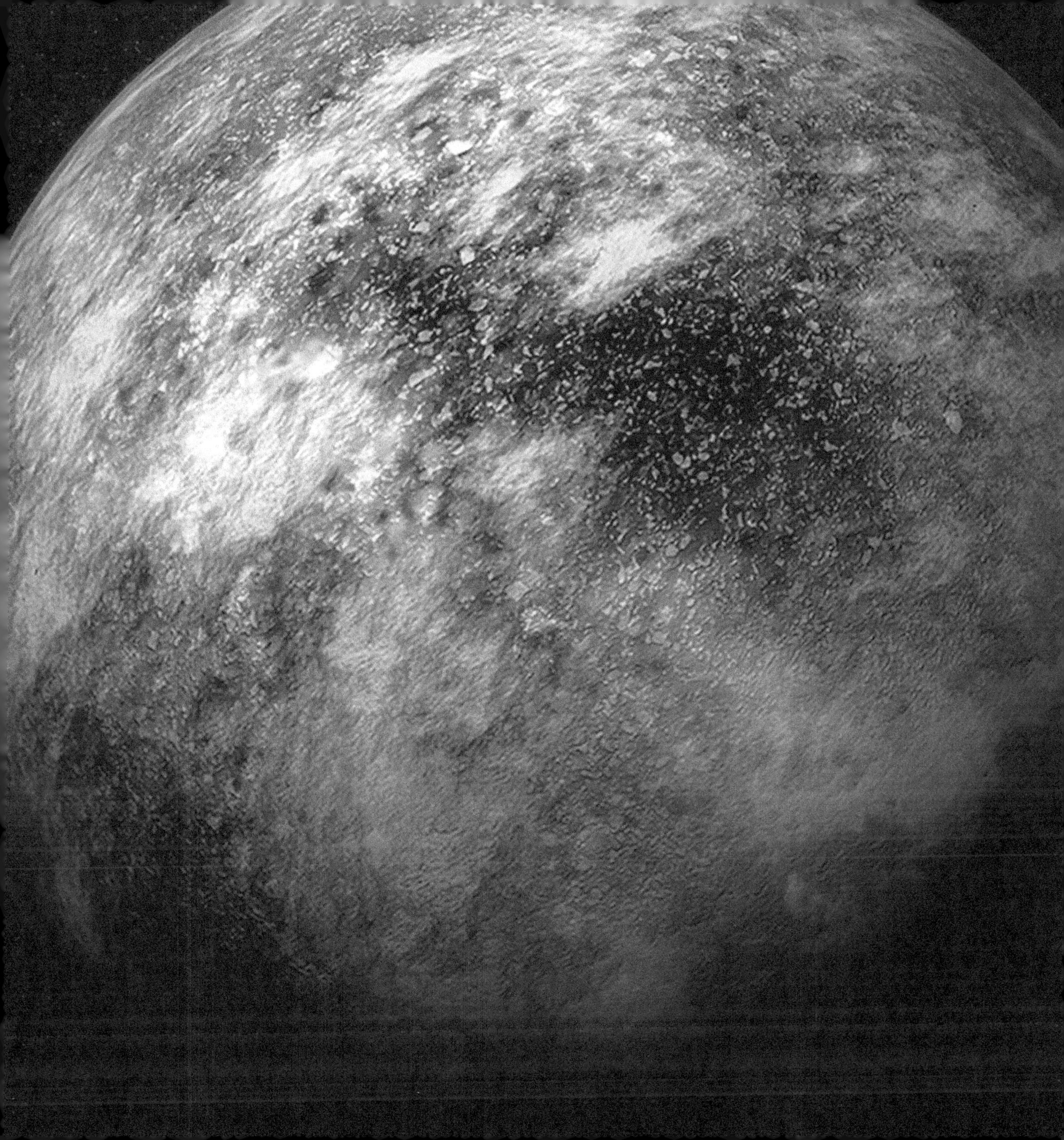

During the time that Pluto is closer to the Sun at 2.8 billion miles, its surface melts and the nitrogen and methane gases go up creating a thin atmosphere. As it gets farther away from the Sun at 4.6 billion miles, the surface freezes back up and the atmosphere decreases and possibly disappears completely.

When compared to the North Star, Earth rotates from west to east. The other planets in our Solar System also rotate from west to east. Pluto rotates from east to west, which means it has a retrograde rotation.

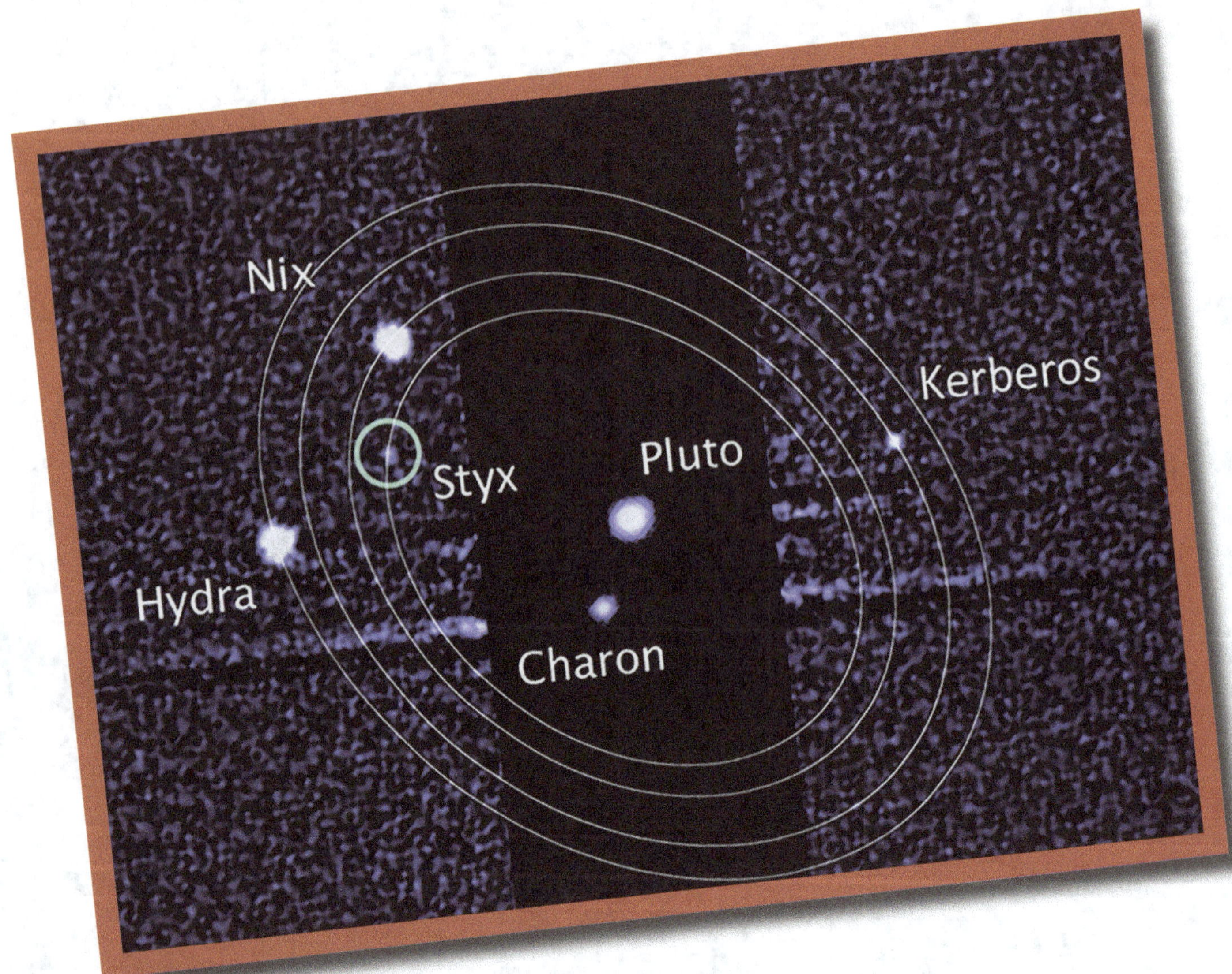

Nix
Kerberos
Styx
Pluto
Hydra
Charon

THE MOONS OF PLUTO

Pluto has five moons.

- Charon, discovered in 1978
- Nix, discovered in 2005
- Hydra, discovered in 2005
- Kerberos, discovered in 2011
- Styx, discovered in 2012

Charon was named after the demon who took souls to hell in the myths told by the Ancient Greeks. Because Charon and Pluto are like twins in terms of size, they have a very unusual orbit. Similar to the way binary stars orbit, Pluto and Charon actually orbit a location in space that is positioned between the two of them.

PLUTO AND CHARON

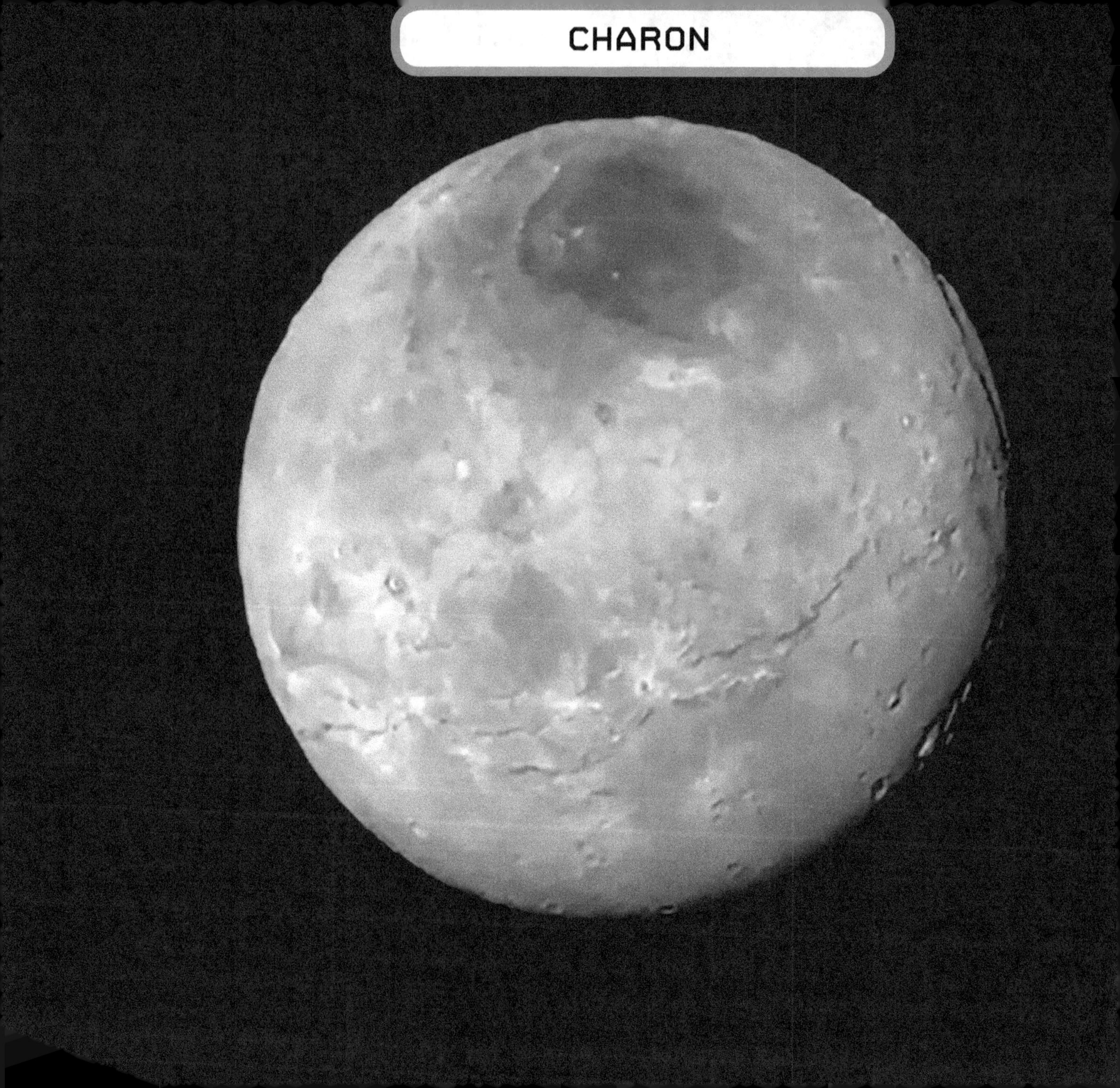

CHARON

These bodies are just about 12,000 miles apart. That's about the distance between London, England and Sydney, Australia on Earth. Charon's orbit around the dwarf planet takes 6.4 days in Earth time. Pluto makes one complete rotation in the same amount of time. This means that Charon always has the same side facing Pluto. This is known as tidal locking.

Compared with the other planets and their accompanying moons in the Solar System, Pluto and Charon are tipped on their sides in relationship to the Sun.

Charon's surface is smooth with no crater marks. It does have very deep canyons that go downward from the surface about 6 miles.

NEW HORIZONS

RESEARCH AND EXPLORATION

The New Horizons mission has been the first one to travel the far distance to the dwarf planet. Because scientific knowledge about Pluto wasn't complete, the spacecraft was put in a dangerous situation.

It had been launched before the moons of Kerberos and Styx had been found. It could have collided with these moons or other debris in orbit around Pluto. Luckily, the spacecraft had special tools to protect it during its long journey to the dwarf planet.

Pluto
Charon
Orcus
Ixion

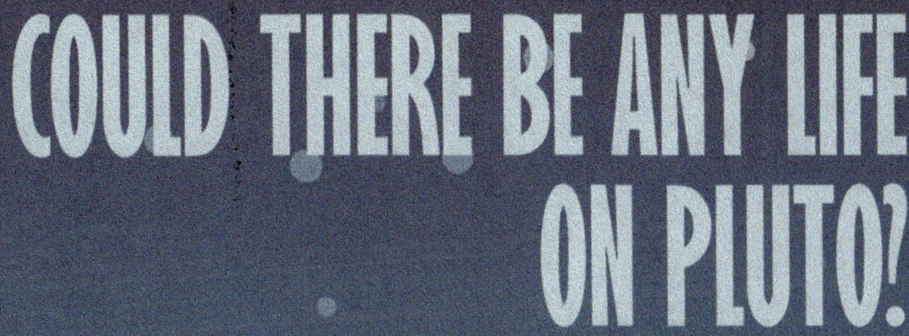

COULD THERE BE ANY LIFE ON PLUTO?

There's very little chance that any life, at least any that resembles ours, exists on Pluto. Even though there is water in the form of ice and organic compounds, the temperature is so cold that it isn't likely.

However, scientists once thought that no life could exist in the volcanic vents at the bottom of Earth's oceans due to the intense heat. Now we know that bacteria can exist at those temperatures, so there is a chance that some type of life has evolved to withstand the icy temperatures there.

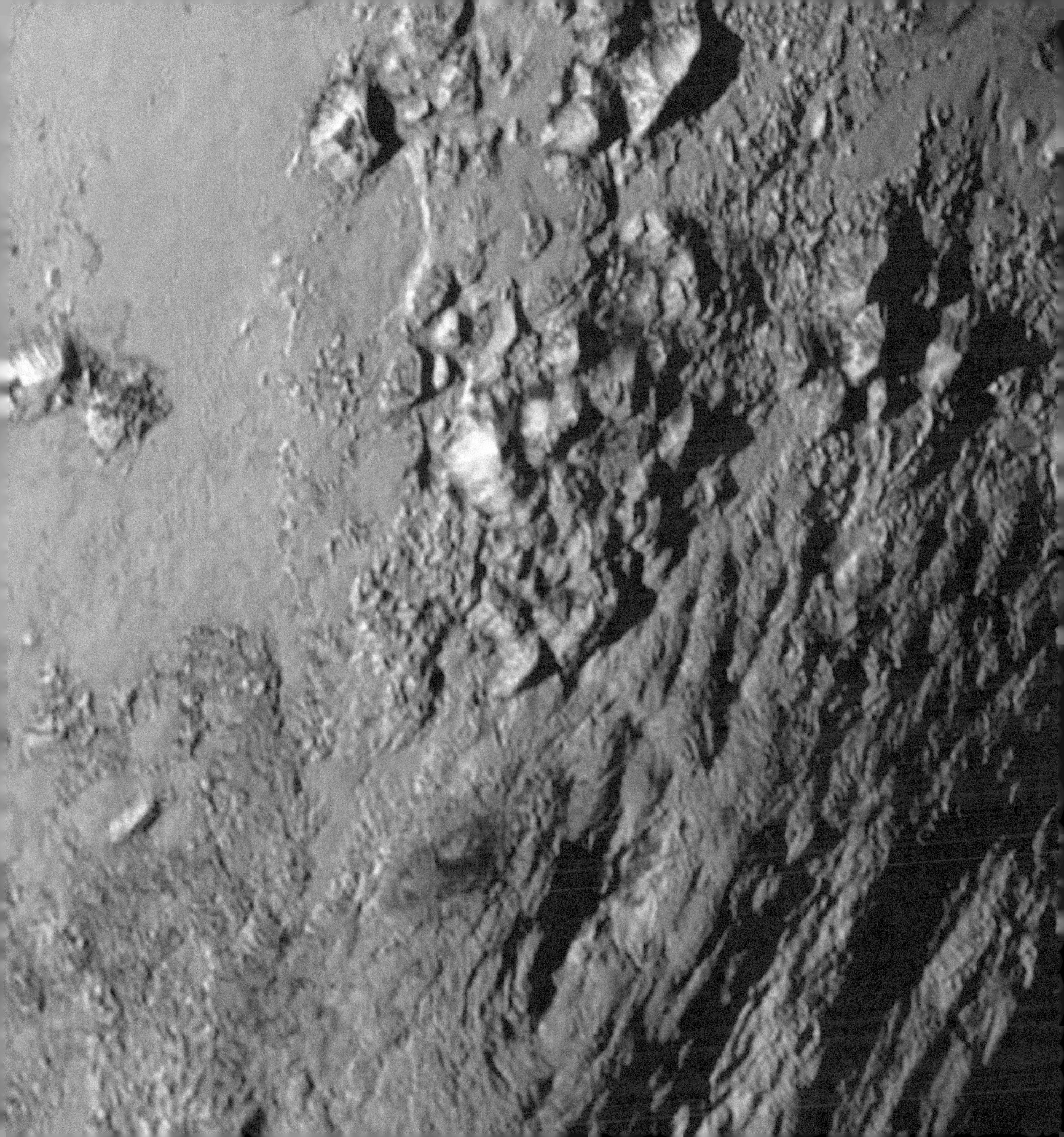

Awesome! Now you know more about the dwarf planet Pluto. You can find more Astronomy books from Baby Professor by searching the website of your favorite book retailer.

Visit
BABY PROFESSOR
EDUCATION KIDS
www.BabyProfessorBooks.com
to download Free Baby Professor eBooks
and view our catalog of new and exciting
Children's Books

www.ingramcontent.com/pod-product-compliance
Lightning Source LLC
Chambersburg PA
CBHW081355150726
48196CB00005BA/503